Vault To Success:
A Beginner's Guide To Altcoin Trading

Table Of Contents

Chapter 1: Introduction to Blockchain & Cryptocurrencies

Chapter 2: Understanding Altcoins

Chapter 3: How to Trade (Buy, Sell, And Swap) Altcoins?

Chapter 4: Trading Crypto Currencies & Understanding the Market

Chapter 5: Protecting your Valuable Crypto Assets

Preface

Many people are hesitant about dealing in cryptos because they do not understand the concept of digital currency or have heard rumors about it. However, there is no need to be hesitant. If you know the basics of cryptocurrency through research, one can gain knowledge about trading securely, about investing diligently, and about being aware of scams. Cryptocurrency is not tangible like fiat currency (you cannot feel cryptocurrency by touching it or having it in your pocket), yet one cannot ignore its impact today in the financial sector.

As a youngster, I was also among the billions who knew nothing of cryptocurrency. I was on the lookout for something stimulating and different and ultimately found crypto trading.

About the Author

Cryptocurrencies have always fascinated me. Trading in altcoins is not just a way of earning money, but it's a passion for me. After much research, and investing my time in this domain, I realized that the lack of adequate knowledge prevented people from investing and trading in crypto. My trading experience in crypto for more than three years could help people clear their doubts and fears, thereby generating interest in crypto trading. Crypto trading has thankfully kept me away from the dreaded 9-to-5 life as I can now trade from virtually anywhere. It may come as a surprise to know that I earned my first crypto fortune while using the bathroom (more on this in the chapters to follow). The initial success inspired me to keep trading in crypto.

I desire to educate people about crypto trading so that they throw the monkey off their backs and begin trading in crypto with newfound confidence. This e-book **Vault To Success: A Beginner's Guide To Altcoin Trading** is a book on trading in altcoins and is a humble beginning in this direction.

My success in crypto trading was achieved through trial and error. I felt that my experience could come in handy for people interested in crypto trading, especially those who want to start with crypto trading but have no idea where to start. Here the seed was sown of writing an e-book on Altcoin trading from which everyone could benefit. I wanted people to identify with me and have therefore interspersed the contents of this book with real-life incidents that everyone could relate to. I hope that these real-life anecdotes would pique your interest in cryptocurrency and convince you to trade in Altcoins. This e-book aims to explain Altcoins in detail and teach you how to trade in them safely while steering clear of all the scams that could come your way.

And, let me tell you about myself. I'm **Patrick** and all my life I've known a couple of things.

- I want to work for myself.
- I want to make the rules.
- I want to make my schedule.

And, I've always invested. Whether it's old comic books, sports cards, or even rare PEZ dispensers; investing has been in my blood and it led me to cryptocurrency.

Introduction

Trading in cryptocurrency can be fun, provided you know what it entails. However, the most challenging aspect of crypto trading is that there are no formal guidelines. Though a lot of literature and relevant information is available on the subject, most of it is so technical that understanding it can be challenging even for a crypto professional. So, if one is an amateur dabbling in this field, one would be left clueless about how to proceed in crypto projects.

I have concluded that people do not trade in cryptocurrency primarily because of one reason, viz. lack of awareness. Though there is a lot of information about

Bitcoin and other major cryptocurrencies like Ethereum, not many people are aware that different types of cryptos also exist. This e-book introduces blockchain and cryptocurrencies without using much technical language that even a beginners can understand. The first chapter deals with these aspects and gradually propels one into learning about Altcoins and how to trade in them.

While cryptocurrencies like bitcoins and altcoins are challenging to comprehend, trading in altcoins is easier because it lacks volatility. On the other hand, Bitcoin trading can be exasperating because the value of Bitcoin changes by the minute. Fluctuating the Bitcoin values often means that one could complete a deal in the morning only to regret it that night because one had not waited for a couple of hours more for a better price. Welcome to the crypto game.

Besides understanding the cryptocurrency market, people should know how to protect their valuable crypto assets as well. This e-book familiarizes the reader with pitfalls like crypto scams which can empty the crypto wallet in no time. This book provides deep insights into the difficulties one faces while trading in cryptocurrency. A complete perusal of this handbook can make one competent enough to deal in cryptocurrency and make a living out of it.

Chapter 1:

Introduction to Blockchain & Cryptocurrencies

1.1   What is Blockchain?

1.1.1 What are Blocks?

1.1.2 Hash, Hash Pointers, and Linked Lists

1.1.3 What is a Chain?

1.1.4 Nodes and Peer to Peer Mechanisms

1.2   Benefits of Blockchain Technology

1.3   What are Crypto Currencies?

1.3.1 Benefits of Cryptocurrencies

1.3.2 Demerits of Cryptocurrencies

1.3.3 Understanding Altcoins and Different Types of Cryptocurrencies

1.4   Understanding Bitcoin

1.5   Bitcoin Mining and Transactions Explained in Brief Conclusion

Blockchain is a revolutionary new technology that can make investors very rich. However, understanding the details of projects and making profitable trades can be pretty tricky, even for veterans. Like many others, I, too, felt lost when I first started learning about cryptocurrencies. Unfortunately, there are too many sources of information to choose from and no shortage of scams seeking to defraud naïve investors. I thankfully never fell victim to these scams, but I know some unfortunate people who did. On the other hand, I also know many crypto "whales" – once ordinary people who are now multimillionaires and enjoy financial freedom due to their investments.

Seeing how cryptocurrency changes peoples' lives prompted me to write this book so others can benefit from the most significant economic development of the 21st century. A lack of knowledge can be dangerous in the wild west of the crypto world, so I wanted investors to understand pitfalls like: Pump and Dump scams, market manipulations, phishing, key thefts, and more. This "Guide to Altcoin Trading" will help beginners get a well-rounded understanding of blockchain, cryptocurrencies, and the fundamentals of trading altcoins. I hope this book gives you, the reader, a head start in cryptocurrency, enabling them to make intelligent investments and enjoy financial freedom.

1.1 What Is Blockchain?

A blockchain can be defined as a decentralized digital ledger that organizes data into chronologically arranged blocks secured using cryptography. Blockchain technology allows the transfer of funds without using the banking system and lets users store information in an immutable secure manner.

You can understand blockchain by thinking of it as a decentralized ledger where data "blocks" are "chained" together using hashing cryptography. We will learn more by looking at the concepts of "Blocks" and "Chaining" separately.

1.1.1 What are Blocks?

Blocks can be thought of as pages in an accountant's ledger. Every "block" here is a container data structure that has information related to a transaction. Bitcoin blocks, for example, are of 1 MB size and store over 500 transactions on average. A block consists of a block header and a block body that contains the transactions.

The block header has six components, which include:

- Block Version Number.
- Previous Block's Hash.
- Merkle Tree Root Hash.
- Current Timestamp.
- Current Difficulty Target
- Variable Nonce.

1.1.2 Hash, Hash Pointers, and Linked Lists

Hash: Hashes are functions that convert inputs of any length to an encrypted output of a fixed size. Using a hash provides security as a particular input always produces the same output, but any slight change to this input drastically changes the output. Bitcoin uses SHA-256 (Secure Hashing Algorithm 256), which has outputs of 256 bits.

Hash Pointers: Pointers are variables that store other variables' addresses and "point" to their location. Hash pointers also contain the hash of the data of a previous block.

Linked List: Linked lists are a kind of data structure consisting of a sequence of blocks where a new block is connected to the previous one using a pointer.

1.1.3 What is a Chain?

The blockchain is a linked list where new blocks have a hash pointer that points to a previous block, thereby creating a "chain" made out of blocks. Since hash pointers contain the hash of the last block, blockchains are immutable. If a hacker tried to change a block's transaction information maliciously, it would change the previous block's hash, and the one before it, and so on. Such change involves redoing the entire work and requires computing power greater than 50% of the network's miners. Considering the Bitcoin network's size and strength, that is pretty much impossible for attackers, thus giving Bitcoin its famous security and immutability.

1.1.4 Nodes and Peer to Peer Mechanisms

Blocks are stored in the hard disks of every full running node of a blockchain's network. This network is maintained by several computers worldwide, thus creating a decentralized ledger. A node here refers to a computer that transmits information within the blockchain network using peer-to-peer protocols. Nodes in a network communicate to ensure that they are on the same block and help ensure the network's security. You, too, can set up a full node.

1.2 Benefits Of Blockchain Technology

Blockchain has several features that make it revolutionary. The key benefits of the technology include:

- **Programmable**: A Blockchain can be thought to be a global computer that can be built for several purposes such as cryptocurrency, smart contracts, decentralized storage, the Internet of Things, and more.

- **Secure**: All transactions in blockchain are encrypted with a Private Key and a Public Key. Blockchain offers high levels of security.

- **Anonymous**: Blockchain protects the identity and privacy of its participants. Both your and the opposing party's identity remains anonymous or pseudonymous.

- **Trustless**: Unless all the network participants agree to the validity of the records, they do not get authenticated. Hence, decentralized, trustless unanimity is a crucial characteristic of blockchain.

- **Immutable**: Once a transaction gets verified and becomes part of the blockchain, it cannot be reversed or altered. Therefore, Blockchain records are immutable.

- **Transparent**: All network participants have a copy of the ledger. This feature enhances transparency and prevents chances of fraud.

1.3 What are Crypto Currencies?

Cryptocurrencies are a class of digital assets based on blockchain technology. Like fiat currencies, they serve as both a medium of exchange and a store of value. However, unlike the dollar, many cryptocurrencies are deflationary and have a limited supply.

Suppose you have $1000 today and then buy groceries with it. Unfortunately, this amount will not get you the same amount of groceries after ten years due to inflation. Fiat currencies thus lose value, but cryptocurrencies like Bitcoin have a limited supply and gain value over time.

1.3.1 Merits of Cryptocurrencies

Some merits of cryptocurrencies include:
- *Confidentiality*: governments do not track them
- *Portability*: they are digital and easily movable
- *Divisibility*: the currencies are highly divisible into smaller units
- *Inflation Resistance*: cryptocurrencies increase in value over time

1.3.2 Demerits of Cryptocurrencies

The Demerits of cryptocurrencies include:

- *Volatile Prices*: prices can be volatile
- *Lack of Regulation*: there are not many laws and regulations compared to other assets
- *Cybersecurity Risks*: people may fall victim to scams if they don't follow best practices

1.3.3 Understanding Altcoins and Different Types Of Cryptocurrencies

All coins other than Bitcoin are known as Altcoins. Altcoins fall into two broad categories, namely coins, and tokens.

Some altcoins include:

- **Ethereum**: Ethereum is a Proof-of-Stake cryptocurrency that has the second-largest market cap after Bitcoin. It allows smart contracts, global payments, decentralized finance, decentralized apps, and more.
- **Litecoin**: An early Bitcoin spinoff, Litecoin is nearly identical to Bitcoin. It decreases block generation time to 2.5 minutes compared to

Bitcoin's 10 minutes, has more maximum coins, and a different hashing algorithm.

- **Ripple**: Ripple is an open-sourced protocol that supports tokens representing fiat money, commodities, and other units of value. It seeks to enable instant free global financial transactions.
- **Cardano**: Cardano is a cryptocurrency similar to Ethereum in that it is Proof-of-Stake. It is based on peer-reviewed research and evidence-oriented methods.

1.4   Understanding Bitcoin

Bitcoin is the first cryptocurrency to gain significant traction. It rose in value from $0 in 2009 to $0.08 in 2010, to $62,000 in 2021. This cryptocurrency was released in 2009 by a pseudonymous personality – Satoshi Nakamoto. Bitcoin's founder wished to create a better, alternative form of currency after the financial collapse of 2008.

Bitcoins are mined using the SHA-256 protocol, and users need a Bitcoin Wallet to hold them after buying from peers, crypto ATMs, or exchanges. These can be

Internet-connected online "hot wallets" or secure cold storage hardware wallets for storing more significant amounts. The merit of Bitcoin is that it holds value, being the most trusted blockchain technology. However, altcoin projects have a more significant earning potential.

1.5 Bitcoin Mining and Transactions Explained in Brief

Suppose you wish to send your friend 3 Bitcoins. First, your device will broadcast a message with the transaction information to all the miners. This message contains:

- Your friend's address
- Intended transaction value - 3 Bitcoins
- A public key
- Secure digital signature made with a private key.

Once miners ascertain the validity of your transaction, they put it in a block with other transactions and attempt to mine it using SHA-256. Miners try to get a hash value lower than the target present in the header. Block headers have five constants and a variable called the nonce. The nonce is raised by one until the miner receives a hash lesser than the target.

> May 22 is known as Bitcoin Pizza Day because a man paid 10,000 bitcoins for a single pizza. Today, the amount translates to more than $3.5 billion. At that time, the value of 10,000 bitcoins was $41.

If a miner is successful, they will broadcast this block to other miners, who check its validity, and then the block is then added to the blockchain with the hash of the previous block. The transaction is then complete. Such Proof-of-Work mining is advantageous as it prevents scams but is very energy-intensive. Proof-of-Stake mining, as in Ethereum, is not energy-intensive but favors already prominent players and can be more susceptible to scams.

1.6 Conclusion

Blockchain technology has the potential to change both the world and the lives of early investors such as you – it has for many before! Investors need to understand the risks and benefits before venturing into the market, and knowing the basics of terminology and the technology is a must.

Chapter 2:
Understanding Altcoins-
"The $10,000 Toilet Trade"

2.1 What are Altcoins?

>*2.1.1 How do Altcoins Work?*

>*2.1.2 Types of Altcoins*

2.2 Altcoins vs. Bitcoin: Advantages and Disadvantages

2.3 Common Terminologies to Know Before Trading

2.4 How to Trade Altcoins

2.5 Risks To Avoid

2.6 Conclusion

I've always day traded and swing traded altcoins for profit. One of the craziest trades was when I tossed $115 into an altcoin after some research. At the time, I had thought that as all the fundamentals were strong, the coin could be enormous. After some time had passed by, I forgot all about this small trade.

Now one day, I was in the bathroom, checking my trades because – believe it or not, I do a lot of trading while in the bathroom – when I suddenly remembered the coin I had put $115 into. So, I thought to myself, "Ah, I'll check it and see how it's doing."

So here I am in the bathroom, trying to check on my investment using awful WiFi speed, and what do I find? My initial $115 investment was now worth over $13,000! Let me tell you – I lost my mind right there. I quickly tried to get a better WiFi signal to lock in the trade.

Time seemed to be slowing down, and the slow WiFi certainly wasn't helping, but in the end, I ended up making the sale for $13,725. The entire experience was one wild trip. After learning from this experience, I recreated my success in future trades by following the same research methods as on this initial coin. Thankfully, I was in a better position, both location and network-wise, during these trades.

This next chapter will discuss the details of altcoins, types, their advantages over bitcoin, risks to avoid, and more so you too can eventually identify trades that earn you five figures off a couple of hundred dollars investment. First, let's begin with understanding what altcoins are.

2.1 What are Altcoins?

There are over 9000 cryptocurrencies as of June 2021. All of them, except Bitcoin, can be termed as an "altcoin." The word altcoin is a portmanteau of "alternative" – i.e., an alternative to Bitcoin – and "coin."

> Namecoin was the first altcoin and was launched in April 2011, two years after Bitcoin's launch.

2.1.1 How do Altcoins Work?

As this is the case with Bitcoin, most of the altcoins do not rely on the government or financial institutions to function. Instead, they can be bought from online exchanges depending on availability, and their prices are determined by the buyers and sellers trading them.

Altcoins usually do not require mediators or agencies to facilitate transactions or store them. Instead, a private key enables users to conduct transactions to and fro through each other's wallets. These transactions are permanently recorded in a public ledger on the blockchain in an immutable and unalterable way. All this being said, every project is different.

2.1.2 Types of Altcoins

Altcoins come in various types depending on the project ideology, target industry, and goals. Some of the main types of altcoins are discussed below.

- **Stablecoins**: These are pegged to another commodity or currency such that their value reflects said item. For instance, Tether (USDT), USDC, and Dai are pegged to the US dollar.

- **Proof-of-Work Mining Coins**: These are created by computers solving complex algorithms. They utilize energy and are generally more secure. - Bitcoin, Monero, etc.

- **Proof-of-Stake Coins**: These coins are pre-minted or forged and distributed rather than mined. Examples are Ripple which is part of Ethereum.

- **Security Tokens**: Security tokens are liquid, digital investment contracts for fractions of assets that already have value, like stocks and real estate. They have regulatory backing.

- ***Utility Tokens:*** Utility tokens are used within a blockchain ecosystem for receiving a service. Examples include the ERC20 Ethereum standard and Sia, a cloud storage P2P solution.

- ***Non-Fungible Tokens (NFTs):*** Bitcoin is a fungible token in that all Bitcoins are identical. NFT, however, have non-identical identification codes. They can be used for unique video game skins, digital artwork, etc. These are also in trend these days, as you have heard of at least one person sending his decade-old meme for thousands of dollars. That was nothing but NFT.

Tokens vs. Coins

Coins have a standalone, independent blockchain. Tokens, however, are derived from other blockchains and don't have a blockchain network of their own. Therefore, tokens being securities, have more robust regulations.

2.2 Altcoins vs. Bitcoin: Advantages and Disadvantages

Many altcoins were created to address the shortcomings of the Bitcoin network and are thus better than it technically. Other altcoins solve entirely different problems, and comparing them to Bitcoin would not be fair.

Pros of Altcoins:

Some pros of altcoins include:

- *Eco-friendliness*: Bitcoin consumes a tremendous amount of energy with a higher block time. PoS altcoins consume no power.

- *Higher Transaction Speeds*: Bitcoin has lower transaction speeds than several other cryptocurrencies.

- *More Earning Potential*: Compared to some Altcoins, Bitcoin may have already expended its initial earning potential.

- ***More Scope***: Altcoin projects have a greater scope as they seek to help make decentralized internet, smart contracts, Internet of Things, decentralized storage, content licensing, and more.

- ***Diversification and Hedging***: Altcoins serve as a hedge against the risk of Bitcoin collapsing due to unforeseen situations.

Cons of Altcoins:

Some cons of altcoins include:

- ***More Volatility***: Altcoins are traditionally more volatile than Bitcoin and thus offer a higher risk-reward scenario.

- ***Need to Watch Out For Scams***: Some altcoins are untested and can lead users to fall victim to pump and dump scams, market manipulations, and so on.

- ***Lack Of Exposure And Acceptance***: Several altcoins have limited exposure, liquidity, and acceptance among retailer investors compared to Bitcoin.

2.3 Common Terminologies to Know Before Trading

Before you start trading altcoins and make big profits, you must know some community-specific jargon so that you don't have problems while "doing your own research (DYOR)" into what coins to trade.

- *Mining:* It is the process of verifying transactions between users and adding them to a blockchain public ledger. Mining is energy-intensive.

- *FOMO:* Fear of missing out (FOMO) on a trading or investment opportunity when an asset rises in value over a short time can cause people to make wrong investment decisions.

- *FUD*: FUD or "Fear, uncertainty, and doubt" is spoken about in the community to describe the act of some users causing uncertainty among others by spreading misinformation or disinformation.

- **Shilling**: Like FUD, the shilling is an act where an organized group of users knowingly or unknowingly promote a coin. It can be either maliciously done for a Pump and Dump Scam or benign to promote their holdings.

- **Wallets**: Crypto wallets allow users to send and receive currencies and generate new blockchain addresses. Wallets can be online "Hot Wallets" that contain small amounts and are used for daily transactions or hardware "cold-storage" devices that store large quantities securely.

- **ICOs**: Similar to an IPO, ICOs or "Initial Coin Offerings" raise capital for a cryptocurrency project. ICOs can be a way of making a lot of money but need due diligence to avoid scams.

- **Private & Public Keys**: A private key is usually a secure Mnemonic phrase that allows one to access their funds. "Not your keys, not your coins" is a famous phrase in the community and signifies how vital ownership of private keys is. A public key allows people to send crypto assets to the receiver.

2.4 How to Trade Altcoins

To begin trading an altcoin, you need first to choose an exchange that is appropriate for your needs and then fund it. Exchanges may be centralized, i.e., with intermediaries or decentralized with direct transactions between users. For example, Kraken, Coinbase, and Binance are some of the most popular cryptocurrency exchanges that are generally used. However, a lot of purchasing takes place on decentralized exchanges (DEX) such as Pancake Swap (a DEX based on Binance Smar Chain) and Uniswap (An Ethereum based DEX) which you will be reading in the following chapters of the book. Keep the following points in mind for your convenience:

- ***Location And Restrictions***: It is wise to choose an exchange that is accessible from your country and is legal.

- ***Liquidity And Volume***: Large market cap coins are better traded at large centralized exchanges and smaller ones at decentralized exchanges.

- ***Safety, Support, KYC***: Centralized exchanges may have better customer support while decentralized ones are more anonymous. For Two factor authentication, avoid SMS if possible as these can be intercepted.

- ***Is Your Altcoin Listed***: Some altcoins are listed only on certain exchanges, so check if an exchange has your chosen altcoin.

2.5 Risks to Avoid

There are several crypto strategies for earning big profits which will be examined later. Here we look at common risks to avoid:

- ***Avoid FOMO and FUD***: Trends are good to make quick money but avoid being influenced by "gurus" who don't know the fundamentals themselves. There is a lot of shilling and FUD in the crypto world, and you have to do your own research.

- ***Manage Risks Effectively***: Learn how to use tools like stop losses to prevent significant losses. Diversify, and don't put all your eggs in one basket. A cardinal investment rule is not investing what you are not ready to lose.

- ***Avoid Phishing and Keep Keys Safe***: Learn the different cybersecurity threats related to crypto projects like market manipulations from whales, pump and dump, phishing, and more. Never give your private keys to anyone!

2.6 Conclusion

Altcoin trading can be very profitable and can eclipse the money that people can now make by investing in Bitcoin. New investors can leverage the volatility to earn money every day, or they can hold projects that they deem worthy and reap the rewards later. Learn the terminologies of the community, do your own research, and know the risks involved before trying out strategies and making your first few thousands in altcoin trading.

Chapter 3: How To Trade (Buy, Sell, and Swap) Altcoins?

3.1 Why is Trading Altcoins Extremely Profitable?

3.2 How to Invest in Altcoins: Using Uniswap, Pancake Swap, and their Benefits

3.3 How to set up Uniswap and Pancake Swap

3.3.1 How to cash out Altcoins?

3.3.2 How to Buy Altcoins; Explained Using Examples – Kishu inu, Shiba inu, and Hoge finance

3.4 A Step By Step Guide on using Trust Wallet And Coinbase Wallet

3.4.1 Steps for using the Trust Wallet

3.4.2 Steps for using Coinbase Wallet

3.5 How to Copy and Paste Contract Addresses Safely

Understanding the fundamentals of trading and building a portfolio took me a long time. Funnily enough, one of the very first cryptos I bought was a meme coin called DOGE. Now Dogecoin doesn't have solid fundamentals, and I wouldn't recommend it now, but at the time, I just bought it because it was affordable.

Time went by, and I honestly forgot all about that little investment. Over three years, I researched a lot about trading, met some influential people, and built an *incredible portfolio that we will be discussing in the next chapter. Now, back to the Dogecoin - It so happened that I was going to Hawaii for vacation and ended up finding the DOGE just a little while before leaving for the trip. That $50 I forgot about for three years? It was worth over $2,000 now!*

I cashed out my returns, bought a drone, a GoPro, and headphones for the flight. A great way to make accidental money, eh? Lol. However, it was like a rare jackpot, and jackpots don't just happen every day! Understanding the market is necessary to succeed in crypto. So, let's dive in!

3.1 Why Trading Altcoin can be Extremely Profitable?

There are several reasons why trading altcoins can be even more profitable than trading Bitcoin.

- **Scope:** Altcoin projects seek to solve several world issues beyond the standard "alternative to fiat currency" Bitcoin aims to achieve. These include: genuinely innovative projects in smart contracts, decentralized finance (DeFi), merchandise originality, logistics, the Internet of Things, and others, to name a few.

- ***Multiplying Profits Several Times***: Bitcoin can easily double or triple your investment, but this scope reduces as it increases in market cap. Think of Bitcoin as a large-cap Bluechip enterprise like Amazon: It multiplied people's investments several hundred times when it was relatively small. However, as Amazon grew in market cap, it was valued more for its stability and staying power. Similarly, small-cap Altcoins can increase your investments several hundred times.

- ***Faster Payments***: Ever since its launch, Bitcoin has suffered from some scalability issues. These can be solved using the lightning network or adoption from organizations like Paypal and Square. But problems persist as no one wishes to sell their Bitcoin. Newer cryptocurrencies or altcoins are designed from the ground up to solve scalability without sacrificing security.

- ***Altcoin Rallies Follows Bitcoin***: Bull markets have consistently witnessed <u>uptrends in altcoins</u> following the uptrend of Bitcoin. Whenever Bitcoin has reached an all-time high, it starts to decline to a new stable point, following which people shift their Bitcoin gains to altcoins that then rise in value. This pattern will likely be repeated in the future.

- ***Affordable Alternatives***: Many undervalued altcoins exist that are an excellent substitute for Bitcoin. They are flexible and have the potential to undergo a significant uptrend as their adoption grows over time. For example, Ethereum is the leader in smart contracts, but as the <u>gas fees of Ether increase</u>, users may adopt alternatives. Being cheaper means the alternatives can increase in price.

- ***Institutional Adoption:*** Growing interest from financial entities like PayPal in cryptocurrencies is excellent for their value. Hedge funds and other entities choose cryptos to diversify their cryptocurrency portfolios. Several <u>Institutional investors consider cryptocurrencies</u> to be a suitable hedge against inflation and catastrophic government monetary policies, thus providing a tremendous boost for altcoins.

3.2 How to Invest in Altcoins: Using Uniswap, Pancake Swap, etc., and their Benefits

When you want to buy altcoins, you will need a crypto exchange. These can either be centralized or decentralized exchanges (DEX) like Uniswap and Pancake swap. A decentralized exchange abbreviated as DEX, in short, is a peer-to-peer (P2P) cryptocurrency marketplace that connects various cryptocurrency buyers and sellers on a common platform. Transactions happen between peers without a middleman or intermediary broker. In contrast to centralized platforms (CEX), decentralized exchanges (DEXs) are non-custodial in functioning, i.e., a user remains in control of their private keys when transacting on a DEX platform.

In the crypto community, it is generally considered better to support decentralization for reasons like:

- *Privacy* – Centralized exchanges ask for KYC information, but users control the private keys on a DEX.

- *Security* – Centralized exchanges are prone to hacking as what happened in the Mt. Gox case.
- *Cheap* – Uniswap charges only 0.3% for any amount
- *More Listings* – More tokens get listed here as centralized exchanges are tightening regulations.

You will also need a crypto wallet. You require an Ethereum wallet to begin trading ERC20 tokens using Uniswap. You can also earn money in Uniswap by providing liquidity to the exchange. PancakeSwap is a competitor that purportedly offers lower fees for faster transactions. DEX's are getting popular, and Uniswap has surpassed Coinbase in trading volume.

Here are a few simple steps:

1. Transfer your FIAT currency (e.g., USD, EUR) to the exchange (e.g., Coinbase, Binance, etc.)

2. Buy some ETH (Ethereum) or you can directly purchase some Cake on Binance.

3. Transfer the required amount of ETH to your personal wallet (e.g., Metamask)

4. Now, you can trade your ETH on UniSwap or Pancake Swap for altcoins after connecting your wallet to it.

3.3 How to set up Uniswap and PancakeSwap

Here we shall take a look at selling altcoins and buying them on DEXs with a few examples.

3.3.1 How to Cash Out Altcoins?

To cash out altcoins, users need to link their wallets with the decentralized exchange or DEX. A detailed guide to withdrawing altcoins using the PancakeSwap DEX is given below:

- To cash out altcoins using PancakeSwap, go to the PancakeSwap exchange website if on a different browser.
- Next, click on 'Currency' under the 'From' tab.
- Copy the contract address of the crypto to be withdrawn and paste it carefully.
- Next, Click on 'Add.'
- Then, under the 'To' tab, Click on BNB.
- Now, scroll down and click on 'Approve.'
- On the next screen, click on 'Swap and Approve.'
- Next, click on 'Swap to Binance Change.'

- Select the percentage that is to be withdrawn.
- Swap coin from 'BEP-20' to 'BEP-2.'
- Now, click on 'Send.'
- Next, go to the exchange and click on 'Deposit.'

3.3.2 Explain by Example how to buy and use Altcoins – Kishu inu, Shiba inu, and Hoge Finance

Kishu Inu, Shiba Inu, and Hoge Finance are some coins similar to DOGE. You can try trading these to get a feel of making your first few crypto trades.

Use the steps below for trading either of these coins on your DEX:

Step 1 - First, ensure that your wallet is connected to Uniswap.

Step 2 - Next, ensure that your wallet contains enough Ethereum to swap. You will need to swap the coins with Ethereum.

Step 3 - If your wallet does not have Ethereum, buy and transfer Ethereum to your wallet.

Step 4 - Next, retrieve the coin's contract address by visiting coinmarketcap.com and searching for 'Kishu Inu.'

Step 5 - Copy the contract address safely; this can be found under the "Contracts" section.

Step 6 - Next, visit app.uniswap.org in your browser or the application.

Step 7 - Click on 'Select a token.'

Step 8 - Here, paste the address of the contract.

Step 9 - Now, the user will find KISHU in the results.

Step 10 - Click on 'Import' against KISHU.

Step 11 - Check the 'I understand' section and click on 'Import.'

Step 12 - Enter the amount to swap.

Step 13 - When you click swap, you will get a confirmation popup including the various fees that would be relevant.

Step 14 - Click on 'Confirm Swap' and the transaction will be processed to swap the Ethereum for Kishu Inu, Shiba Inu, or Hoge finance.

Step 15 - You just learned how to buy your first coin on a DEX!

3.4 A Step by Step Guide on using Trust Wallet And Coinbase Wallet

Apart from a DEX, you will also need a wallet to begin trading. Trust wallet is a Binance smart chain wallet that can be connected to PancakeSwap to earn CAKE bonuses by providing liquidity. It can also be used for swapping currencies. Coinbase, meanwhile, is excellent for beginners.

3.4.1 Steps for using the Trust Wallet

Start by downloading Trust Wallet and launching it. Select 'Create a new wallet' and note your recovery phrase very carefully.

To swap a coin, follow these steps,

- To transfer coins from DEXs to your wallet, open Trust Wallet and choose the coin.
- Copy the wallet address and go to the DEX by searching for it in DApps.

- Select the token to exchange and the location to send it.
- Click on the swap button.
- After this, you can preview the transaction and confirm it.

3.4.2 Steps For Using The Coinbase Wallet

To use the Coinbase Wallet, follow the steps given below.

- Download Coinbase from App Store or Google Play and Launch.
- On the next screen, click on 'Get started.'
- Enter your details and verify your email.
- Read the User Agreement check the box.
- Next, link a payment method.
- To buy crypto, tap the settings icon at the bottom.
- Scroll downwards until 'Transfer' appears and tap on 'Transfer.'
- Next, choose the crypto to invest in and enter the amount.
- Click on 'Continue' and then 'Confirm.'

- If a payment method is added, the remaining prompts can be followed to buy crypto from the wallet.

3.5 How to Copy and Paste Contract Addresses Safely

A contract address is a hexadecimal representation of a 160-bit number and is a unique address on the chain that stores the contract for the transaction. Contract addresses can be found by visiting etherscan.io; a quick search of the preferred coin will show its details. The 'Contract' section contains a contract address. This address can be copied safely as this is a trusted site. You can paste the address while selecting a coin on Uniswap or PancakeSwap.

On the other hand, you see one hyperlink, "View contract," when you click a currency on PancakeSwap. Clicking on the URL will take you to the respective blockchain webpage. Generally, you'll also see a small 'Copy' button ('Copy address to clipboard), and it's safe to use this button so that you do not miss any characters from the long contract address.

Conclusion

There are many ways to buy and store cryptocurrency in the digital age. However, you should consider decentralized methods as these follow the core philosophy behind all crypto projects. In addition, keeping wallets safe should be your primary goal. Investing in altcoins can be risky, and you should do thorough research before investing.

Chapter 4: Trading Crypto Currencies & Understanding the Market

4.1 Building a Foundational Portfolio of Established Cryptos Before Jumping into Altcoins

>*4.1.1 Starting your Crypto Portfolio*

>*4.1.2 Selecting your Crypto Exchange*

>*4.1.3 Some Essential Crypto Security Tips*

4.2 How to Buy BNB, BTC, or ETH with Fiat Currency

4.3 How To Swap Coins With Each Other: BNB, BTC, ETH, and More

4.4 Guide on Buying Crypto and Transferring it to a Wallet: BNB and Trust Wallet

4.5 Difference Between BNB And the Binance Smart Chain

4.6 How to Send and Receive Crypto from One Wallet To Another

Trading in cryptocurrencies is like trading in traditional stocks and bonds. One first needs to carry out due diligence before investing. As there are more than 9000 cryptocurrencies, deciding what to invest in can be overwhelming. Beginners should make a solid foundation with established currencies like Ethereum and start experimenting only with money one is okay with losing. As one's knowledge of the crypto asset class increases, one's portfolio can increase as well. Now, let's get down to the business and start to build a foundational portfolio.

4.1 Building a Foundational Portfolio of Established Cryptos Before Jumping Into Altcoins

Choosing cryptos to get started with can be challenging. There are many coins with potential but an equally large number of purely speculative or fraudulent projects. Beginners should start with the safest option, i.e., Bitcoin. Bitcoin is a necessity for all subsequent investments as several cryptos are better bought directly with Bitcoin rather than with fiat money.

4.1.1 Starting your Crypto Portfolio

If you intend to become a serious investor, you need to also have a few altcoins in your portfolio. Choose a coin that has a lot of active daily trades; it will ensure sufficient liquidity so that you can trade your altcoins as required.

Some of the foundational cryptocurrencies you can get started with are:

- Bitcoin (BTC)
- Ethereum (ETH)
- Cardano (ADA)
- Litecoin (LTC)
- Tether (USDT)

4.1.2 Selecting your Crypto Exchange

While considering a crypto exchange, selecting one that suits the cryptocurrencies you intend to invest in is crucial. Other essential factors to consider are- reasonable transaction fees and robust security. At a later stage, you will need to buy a wide variety of cryptos, so it is crucial to keep that in mind from the beginning.

As the crypto market matures, several reliable and secure exchanges have emerged. According to <u>Forbes</u>, the top five exchanges and their specialties are:

- Binance.us *(Cheapest transactions and good selection of altcoins)*
- Coinbase *(Best for Beginners)*
- Kraken *(Faster withdrawals to banks)*
- Crypto.com *(Discounts on trading fees and other benefits)*
- Gemini *(Simple, easy-to-use interface)*

4.1.3 Some Essential Crypto Security Tips

With cybercrime rising by the day, cryptocurrency <u>theft insurance</u> is something every investor should consider. Apart from that, ensure that the chosen exchange is a secure one. Some things to look for include whether they have a bug bounty, insurance, and cold storage. Crypto.com, Coinbase, and Gemini have these features.

Using a hardware cold storage device from Ledger or Trezor is also highly recommended as these are highly resistant to online hacking. Be warned, though, that if you lose the recovery key, you cannot recover the wallet's contents. You can get your key printed in steel to prevent this. Some cold wallets also allow users to have small "fake" amounts with a different recovery to protect against a physical robbery.

4.2 How to Buy BNB, BTC, or ETH with Fiat Currency

Buying Cryptocurrencies with fiat money is simple if you are willing to share KYC information with an exchange.

In Binance, for example, you can follow the steps below:

- *Step 1:* From the **Buy Crypto** dropdown menu, select Credit/Debit Card or other options.
- *Step 2:* From the **Spend** field, select the currency you want to use – e.g., USD/ EUR (as per your location) – and enter the amount you want to spend.
- *Step 3:* In the **Receive** field, select the crypto coin you want to buy.
- *Step 4:* Review the details, add your Credit Card and complete the transaction

> If you do not want to share KYC, then you might have to exchange hard cash for crypto using services like Localbitcoins, Paxful, or Bitcoin ATMs.

4.3 How to Swap Coins with Each Other: BNB, BTC, ETH, And More

Before swapping coins, you need to check your exchange to see if the crypto you want to receive in the swap process is supported.

To start, you need to have at least one type of coin in your wallet which you want to trade for another kind of crypto. Let's use the Binance crypto exchange in our example.

To swap your coin, follow this step-by-step guide:

- Head over to the **Finance** menu and select **Liquid Swap.**
- Then click on the **"Swap"** tab in the sub-menu. Here you will see two fields – *Sell* (the coin you intend to swap out) and *Buy* (the crypto you want to receive).

- You can then enter how much you wish to sell in the Sell field or how much you wish to receive in the Buy field.
- Confirm your swap amounts and click on "**Swap**" to complete the swap.

Note: Depending on your exchange, there may be some nominal fees for completing a swap.

4.4 Guide on Buying Crypto and Transferring it to a Wallet: BNB and Trust Wallet

If you want to send BNB to Trust Wallet, make sure you have the application installed, registered, and logged in on your Android or iOS device.

Buying BNB on Binance: Buying BNB on Binance can be done on a regular PC.

We have seen how this can be achieved in section 4.2 using one of the supported currencies. However, if you want to buy BNB on the Binance mobile app, the steps given below will help:

- Log in and tap on **Markets**.

- Search for BNB. There are multiple entries listed for BNB. Since we are using USD for buying BNB, locate the option **BNB/USDT** and tap on it. You will now see the current price of BNB.
- Tap on **BUY**. You will be directed to the **Spot** tab.
- Tap on the **Limit** dropdown list and select **Market.**
- Enter the USD you want to spend for buying BNB.
- Tap on **Buy BNB.** You will see a small 'Success' notification. Check the deduction of this amount from your available balance just above the Buy BNB button.

Now that we have purchased some BNB, we are ready to transfer it to Trust Wallet.

- Open up Trust Wallet and scroll down to **Smart Chain** and tap on it.
- Then select the **Receive** option. It will display an address along with a QR code.
- Tap on **Copy** to copy the address.
- Switch to the Binance application. From the **Wallets** section, select **BNB.**
- In BNB details, tap on **Withdrawal** and paste the copied address.

> *Important:* In the **Network** option, select **BEP20 (BSC)**, i.e., the Binance Smart Chain Network.

- Enter the amount of BNB you wish to transfer to Trust Wallet in the Amount field. If you want to transfer all of it, tap on **MAX.**
- Tap on the **Withdrawal** button and then click **Confirm**. You will have to enter the verification code and click on **Submit** to complete the transaction.
- Wait for the order confirmation on the next screen before viewing the history to check the withdrawals.

It can take around two minutes to process the transaction and see the amount reflected in your Trust Wallet.

4.5 Difference Between BNB and the Binance Smart Chain

Binance Coin (BNB) is the Binance cryptocurrency exchange's native token. The Binance ecosystem, formerly built on the Ethereum blockchain, has a dual blockchain structure – the Binance Chain (BC) and the Binance Smart Chain (BSC) that run parallel to each other.

The Binance Chain was built for speed and permissionless trading. It lacks extraneous features and flexibility like smart contract functionality or compatibility with the Ethereum Virtual Machine (EVM).

Meanwhile, the Binance Smart Chain (BSC) supports Ethereum-based DApps (Decentralized Applications) with faster speeds and lower transaction fees. In addition, DApps such as PancakeSwap and BakerySwap, which follow the DeFi (DecentralizedFinance) protocols, are also supported on the Binance Smart Chain network.

With this dual chain running parallelly, users can benefit from the advantages of both the chains, i.e., speed and flexibility. As an additional feature, should either blockchain fail, the other can act as a redundant fallback.

4.6 How to Send and Receive Crypto from one Wallet to Another

Transferring cryptocurrency from one wallet to another can differ slightly between different wallets, but the underlying principles remain the same. Some wallets like Coinbase do not charge any transfer fees but charge Network fees instead, which is a charge that goes to a third party (the miners processing the transaction). Transactions between wallets on the same exchange may not incur any fees at all.

Now, let us look at the basic process of transferring crypto from a sender to a receiver.

- Before a sender initiates a transfer, one needs to have the public address where the crypto needs to be deposited.
- The receiver can provide this to the sender by going to the desired wallet, selecting the asset type (e.g., Bitcoin, Litecoin, etc.), copying the given address, and sending it over to the sender.
- The sender initiates a transaction by going to their wallet and clicking send/withdraw, and then selecting the same asset type as the receiver (here Bitcoin).
- They then paste the receiver's wallet address in the "recipient" address field. Finally, enter the amount of Bitcoin to be transferred. Complete the 2-factor authentication for the transaction to finally proceed.

- Some transfers may incur charges, while others may not, depending on the networks provided by the exchange.

Conclusion

While trading cryptocurrencies is lucrative, beginners must start by building a solid foundational portfolio from which they can start experimenting. Learn the fundamentals of transferring and buying cryptos to get started on making decent profits. There are plenty of altcoins to invest in, but not all of them are great investments. Investing in the right altcoin will require good research, knowing the fundamental concept behind the project, and relying on community support.

Chapter 5: Protecting your Valuable Crypto Assets

5.1 How to Protect Yourself While Trading?

    5.1.1 Knowing What Projects to Invest in, Wisely

    5.1.2 How much to Invest (What You're Willing To Lose)

    5.1.3 Taking Calculated Risks.

5.2 Avoiding Scam Altcoins.

    5.2.1 Using Tokensniffer.com to Wean out Potential Scam Coins

    5.2.2 Securing your Investment During ICOs

    5.2.3 Things to Remember on Telegram Channels and not get Phished

5.3 Securing your Crypto Assets With Best Practices

    5.3.1 Crypto Wallet Best Practices

    5.3.2 Storing your Private Keys Securely

    5.3.3 Password Protection and MFA (Multi-Factor Authentication)

One of the prime features that make Blockchain technology so relevant is the security it offers. All transactions in Blockchain need a private and a public key to work. There are several cryptocurrencies in circulation today that provide transactional anonymity while safeguarding user privacy. If users follow some basic cybersecurity practices, they will probably never lose their coins to some scam. However, several fraudulent projects and pump and dump schemes exist, and you have to be vigilant.

Would you love to have a website that could provide you valuable information about known and ongoing scams or hacking attacks in crypto? tokensniffer.com is among my favorite sites for identifying scam coins. Yes, I know the name sounds like something NSFW, but I promise that researching potential coins on this site will save you tons of money. This site lists various scams as they uncover and keep you updated on what projects to avoid.

All trading in stocks, shares, bullion, or crypto comes with its share of risks. The primary risk of trading in cryptocurrency is volatility. Additionally, as cryptocurrency is still a niche industry, it does not have as many security standards as other sectors, thus increasing risk. However, if you play things intelligently, the maxim of "the higher the risk, the higher the rewards" applies to this sector, as well.

Let us see how you can protect your crypto assets while trading.

5.1 How to Protect Yourself While Trading?

Now that you have familiarized yourself with trading, let's look at how you can protect yourself and your investments in the crypto arena.

5.1.1 Knowing What Projects to Invest in, Wisely

Some people feel that cryptocurrency's scope is restricted only to big projects like Bitcoins, Ethereum, and maybe a handful more. In the community, they are known as maximalists. On the opposite end of the spectrum, thousands of cryptocurrencies exist in the crypto market. Most of these cryptos have no future beyond quick speculative gains.

When you trade, please do thorough research on a coin's community, whitepaper, the social signals, sentiment, and long-term prospects. Short-term trading is always speculative and can be hurt by factors beyond the ability of people to predict. You can adopt a strategy first or copy trades of investors with proven reputations on sites like eToro.

5.1.2 How Much To Invest (What You're Willing To Lose)

When you invest in crypto, there is no guarantee that you will gain money. Unless you know what you are doing, you will make losses and might even lose your entire capital. You might also double it or even multiply it 1000x. This volatility makes trading in cryptos an exciting affair.

One of investing's most significant rules is knowing your loss threshold. In simple words, you should know what amount of loss you can sustain. Anything below that should be a strict "No!" Similarly, in cryptocurrency, know how much to invest, and never invest more than you can lose.

5.1.3 Taking Calculated Risks

Now that you know what to invest in and how much to invest, you can proceed by taking calculated risks. Doing so is possible only if you understand the trends in the industry, and this comes with experience. Make small trades, nothing more than 10% of your available capital, and see how they play out. Set stop losses to limit your loss and risk.

Cryptocurrency can be a highly volatile asset class, with the values touching the sky one moment and falling to all-time lows the next within no time. Besides, as we will see below, you have to be wary of the scams that keep happening all the time. Even a project like Bitconnect caused many to lose hundreds of thousands.

5.2 Avoiding Scam Altcoins

Altcoins are all cryptocurrencies other than Bitcoin. They include: mining-based cryptocurrencies, security tokens, stable coins, proof-of-stake coins, meme coins, utility tokens, and much more. Today, you have several altcoins in the crypto market with Ethereum, Tether, and Binance Coin being the largest by market capitalization.

While you have thousands of altcoins, not all of them are genuine. Let us see how to know whether an altcoin is real or fake.

5.2.1 Using Tokensniffer.com to Wean out Potential Scam Coins

Token sniffer is a popular website that can help you to identify crypto scams. This site maintains a list of all known scams and lets you see tokens with similar mechanics.

Through this website, you would get a good idea of what projects to invest in and which projects to avoid. Tokensniffer.com works with a mission to make DEX trading safe from harmful contracts, exit scams, and other malicious schemes. It also provides a list of trending tokens that can prove helpful for crypto trading.

5.2.2 Securing your Investment During ICOs

Despite claims of all cryptocurrencies being safe for trading, several highly publicized cases reveal that threat actors have broken through even the most stringent security measures at times. Statistics show that nearly 10% of all funds raised by ICOs (Initial Coin Offering) are reported stolen or hacked.

Follow the steps below to secure your ICO investments:

- **Check Developers for Responsiveness**: Users should check if the developers listen to their community and are willing to be guided by it. Good crypto communities usually have many people with relevant knowledge who can keep looking for vulnerabilities in the system. If the developers don't listen to the community, it can lead to incidents like the loss DAO suffered in 2016.

Decentralized Autonomous Organization (DAO) was created to automate and facilitate crypto transactions. In June 2016, hackers attacked DAO and accessed 3.6 million ETH due to programming errors and attack vectors.

- **Protect Against Phishing**: Phishing is a social engineering attack where the attacker gains your trust by pretending to be someone they are not. Learn about how to identify such attacks and avoid them in time to protect yourself.

- **Read about Scams**: You should make yourself more aware of cybersecurity incidents like the CoinDash ICO story when trading in crypto so you can avoid projects that make similar mistakes. One way of preventing such incidents from affecting you is to install a powerful web application firewall.

Hackers exploited a vulnerability in the CoinDash ICO by gaining access to the official website. It allowed them to alter a source file and get complete remote control over the website. By changing the wallet address, these cyber attackers got away with a massive heist.

ICO companies should audit their underlying smart contracts using blockchain security services that focus on security and pen testing for blockchain applications to detect problems. Investors can check if their chosen developer focuses on such security measures. Invest only in ICOs that protect their users and ensure that investors can access their funds.

5.2.3 Things to Remember on Telegram Channels and not get Phished

The Telegram app is extremely popular in cryptocurrency circles, and major crypto communities are on the app.

Protecting yourself on Telegram is critical as chat groups are also prone to phishing attacks.

These steps can help protect your Telegram account:

- **Two-Factor Authentication**: Turn on two-factor account authentication wherever possible. Install a security solution with anti-phishing capability will also help.

- **Unknown Senders**: Be wary of anonymous users contacting you on Telegram with the latest coin going to the "moon." Take all investment advice with a pinch of salt and know the kind of language used by scammers.

- **Sharing Private Information**: Be very careful before entering any information on a web page. Look at the domain name of any site closely, as it can contain spelling errors and be a scam. Don't share passwords, keys, or private info on Telegram.

5.3 Securing your Crypto Assets with Best Practices

The following steps can help you to secure your crypto assets.

5.3.1 Crypto Wallet Best Practices

The best practices for your crypto wallets are:

- Use a cold storage hardware wallet for large sums.
- Avoid public Wi-Fi and use a VPN for additional security.
- Use multiple, trusted wallets and don't keep everything in one wallet.
- Use the latest anti-virus software.
- Changing your password regularly is advisable and optimal for MFA.

5.3.2 Storing Your Private Keys Securely

"Not your keys, not your coins" is a well-known maxim. Here is how you can store your private keys safely.

- **Cold Storage:** The best place to store your private key is in an offline storage device like Ledger or

Trezor. These cold wallets store the keys behind encryption so that they cannot be stolen via the Internet.

- ***Physically Printed Key***: Keys can be physically printed in steel and then kept in the bank locker for additional security.

- ***Use only Trusted Solutions***: Only associate with organizations that are well known in the crypto community, open-source, audited and trusted.

5.3.3 Password Protection and MFA (Multi-Factor Authentication)

Use these tips for proper password protection and MFA

- Employ robust passwords comprising small and large alphabets, special characters, and numbers. A password managing tool can help with this.
- Opt for multi-factor authentication but not via SMS as these can be intercepted easily. Biometric verification to confirm a transaction is a good option.

Avoid using easy-to-guess passwords such as your spouse's name, children's name, date of birth, anniversary dates, or simple number combinations like 123456, 111111, etc. Such passwords are easily guessed. Avoid using the same password for multiple accounts, as a hack on one account can compromise several accounts.

Trading cryptocurrencies can be risky, but it is an enriching endeavor if you maintain proper precautions. It would help if you first got the hang of how the crypto markets function and understand changing trends. Along with this, use appropriate cybersecurity strategies to prevent getting phished by hackers. Secure storage of your keys is critical because coins can get stolen if your keys are lost. Follow all the safety measures discussed above to secure your precious crypto assets and start earning big money in altcoin trading!

Final Words

Trading in crypto can be tricky, especially with the value of cryptocurrencies like Bitcoin touching the sky one day and falling drastically the very next minute. However, other cryptocurrencies, also known as altcoins, are not as volatile. One can make a decent living out of trading in cryptos, provided they have the requisite knowledge on the subject. This e-book goes a long way in educating people on the concept of altcoins and the perils one can face while trading in them. It also highlights the various cryptocurrency scams floating all around the market.

A thorough reading of this e-book will equip one with the proper knowledge of dealing with crypto trading. The chapters have been carefully selected to explain these points in the most straightforward manner possible. As the subject can get a bit dry at times, this book attempts to liven things up by including funny anecdotes at appropriate places. The primary aim of this e-book is that people can learn the basics of crypto trading before venturing into the activity. While making one aware of the benefits of crypto trading, this book also highlights the scams floating around in the field. It also helps people to understand the perils, thereby enabling them to make informed decisions, multiply their capital, and achieve financial freedom!

Thirsty for more? Join my free telegram below and engage in daily crypto conversations with hundreds of members!

References

1. Conway, L. and Mansa, J. June 01, 2021. *Blockchain Explained.*Investopedia.
   https://www.investopedia.com/terms/b/blockchain.asp

2. *What is Blockchain?* Extracted from https://www.euromoney.com/learning/blockchain-explained/what-is-blockchain

3. Kumar, R. December 27, 2013. *Bitcoin explained in layman's terms.* NDTV Profit. https://www.ndtv.com/business/bitcoin-explained-in-laymans-terms-376029

4. Allen, A. November 13, 2017. *What is Bitcoin Mining?* Blockchain. https://www.jumpstartblockchain.com/article/what-is-bitcoin-mining/

5. Frankenfield, J. and Sonnenshein M. May 25, 2021. *What is cryptocurrency?* Cryptocurrency. https://www.investopedia.com/terms/c/cryptocurrency.asp

6. Soni, S. April 03, 2021. *RIP cryptocurrencies: Number of dead coins up 35% over last year; tally nears 2000-mark.* Financial Express. https://www.financialexpress.com/market/rip-cryptocurrencies-number-of-dead-coins-up-35-over-last-year-tally-nears-2000-mark/2226169/

7. Agarwal, H. August 21, 2020. *9 Interesting Bitcoin Facts Every Bitcoin Owner Should Know.* Coin Sutra. https://coinsutra.com/bitcoin-facts/

8. Shen, L. (2018, January 23). *Hackers Have Stolen $400 Million From ICOs.* Fortune. *https://fortune.com/2018/01/22/ico-2018-coin-bitcoin-hack/*

9. Yuval, M. (2017, November 15). *CoinDash TGE Hack Findings Report 15.11.17.* Coindash. *https://blog.coindash.io/coindash-tge-hack-findings-report-15-11-17-9657465192e1*

10. Liebkind, J. (2019, June 25). *ICO Security Playbook: 5 Steps To Ensure Best Practice.* Investopedia.

https://www.investopedia.com/news/ico-security-playbook-5-steps-ensure-success/

11. Reiff, N. (2019, June 25). *What Is A Decentralized Autonomous Organization (DAO)?* Investopedia. *https://www.investopedia.com/tech/what-dao/*

12. Demidova, N. (2018, March 06). *A Wave Of Telegram Hacks Hits: How To Protect Your Account.* Kaspersky Daily. *https://www.kaspersky.co.in/blog/telegram-accounts-stealing/12683/*

13. Srinivas, R. (2020, August 17). *How To Safeguard Your Cryptocurrency Wallet From Digital Exploits.* CISOMAG. *https://cisomag.eccouncil.org/cryptocurrency-wallet-security/*

14. Huddleston, C. April 27, 2021. *What Are Altcoins? – Are The Potential Rewards Worth The Risks?*

https://www.gobankingrates.com/money/economy/economy-explained-what-are-altcoins-and-should-you-invest-in-them/

15. What Does Altcoin Mean? *CFI.* https://corporatefinanceinstitute.com/resources/knowledge/other/altcoin-guide/

16. Bhavishy6. May 12, 2021. *Proof-of-work.* https://ethereum.org/en/developers/docs/consensus-mechanisms/pow/

17. *Hardware Implementation For Fast Block Generator Of Litecoin Blockchain System.* IEEE. https://ieeexplore.ieee.org/abstract/document/9418691/authors#authors

18. *What Is Cryptocurrency Mining?* Binance Academy. https://academy.binance.com/en/articles/what-is-cryptocurrency-mining

19. Ma, J. *Fear Of Missing Out.* Binance Academy.

https://academy.binance.com/en/glossary/fear-of-missing-out

20. Chowdhury, S. *Fear, Uncertainty, And Doubt*. Binance Academy.
https://academy.binance.com/en/glossary/fear-uncertainty-and-doubt

21. April 07, 2021. *Bitcoin Boom Minted Nine New Cryptocurrency Billionaires In One Year*. Mint.
https://www.livemint.com/market/cryptocurrency/bitcoin-boom-minted-nine-new-cryptocurrency-billionaires-last-year-11617781741726.html

22. Qiheng, Z., Huawei. H., Zheng. Z., Bian, J. (2020). *Solutions To Scalability Of Blockchain: A Survey.* IEEE.
https://ieeexplore.ieee.org/stamp/stamp.jsp?arnumber=8962150

23. Croman, K., Decker, C., Eyal, I., Efe Gencer, A., Juels, Ari., Kosba, A., Miller, A., Saxena, P., Shi, E., G¨un Sirer, E., Song, D., Wattenhofer, R. (2016). *On*

Scaling Decentralized Blockchains (A Position Paper). IFCA. *https://fc16.ifca.ai/bitcoin/papers/CDE+16.pdf*

24. De Best, R. (2021). *Bitcoin In Circulation 2009-2021.* Statista. *https://www.statista.com/statistics/247280/number-of-bitcoins-in-circulation/*

25. Chambers, C. (2020). *Why Is Bitcoin Driving Altcoins To The Moon?* Forbes *https://www.forbes.com/sites/investor/2020/01/15/why-bitcoin-driving-altcoins-cyrpto/*

26. De Best, R. (2021). *Ethereum Gas Price 2015-2021.* Statista. *https://www.statista.com/statistics/1221821/gas-price-ethereum/*

27. Tatibouet, M. (2021). *Institutions Investing In Bitcoin Isn't About Money — It's About The Mindset.* Nasdaq.

https://www.nasdaq.com/articles/institutions-investing-in-bitcoin-isnt-about-money-its-about-the-mindset-2021-04-11

28. Leech, O. (2021). *What Is Uniswap? A Complete Beginner's Guide.* Yahoo. *https://in.news.yahoo.com/uniswap-complete-beginner-guide-100917816.html*

29. Nash, M. (2021). *Top 5 Cryptocurrency Decentralized Exchanges.* Washington Independent. *https://washingtonindependent.com/cryptocurrency-decentralized-exchanges/*

30. Vermaak, W. (2021). *Uniswap vs. PancakeSwap.* Coinmarketcap. *https://coinmarketcap.com/alexandria/article/uniswap-vs-pancakeswap*

31. CISOMAG. (2020). *6 Steps For Protecting Your Cryptocurrency Wallet From Malevolent Hands.* CISOMAG.

https://cisomag.eccouncil.org/cryptocurrency-wallet-security/

32. Taylor Tepper, John Schmidt. (2021, May 27). *Best Crypto Exchanges For 2021.* Forbes. *https://www.forbes.com/advisor/investing/best-crypto-exchanges/*

33. The European Business Review. (2021, January 4). *How To Build Your Cryptocurrency Portfolio In 2021.* *https://www.europeanbusinessreview.com/how-to-build-your-cryptocurrency-portfolio-in-2021/*

34. Artem Popov. (2020, January 4). *Low-Volatility Cryptocurrencies: The Different Types, Their Potentials, And The Underlying Technology.* Forbes. *https://www.forbes.com/sites/forbestechcouncil/2020/01/16/low-volatility-cryptocurrencies-the-different-types-their-potentials-and-the-underlying-technology/?sh=35d347262977*

35. Debbie Chia. (2021, February 19). *What Is Binance Smart Chain? BSC And BNB Coin Explained.* Exodus. *https://www.exodus.com/blog/what-is-binance-smart-chain-bnb/*

36. Blockchain Support Center. (2021, June 21). *What Is Swap? https://support.blockchain.com/hc/en-us/articles/360026011331-What-is-Swap-*

37. Coinbase. *Can I Convert My Cryptocurrency To Another Cryptocurrency? https://help.coinbase.com/en/more/coinbase-wallet/getting-started/dex*

38. Binance Blog. (2021, February 24). *Trade, Swap, Or Convert: 3 Ways To Buy Crypto For Binance Launchpool. https://www.binance.com/en/blog/42149982468490 1697/trade-swap-or-convert-3-ways-to-buy-crypto-for-binance-launchpool*

39. Binance Blog. (2021, March 16). *Binance Convert: Making Crypto Transactions Quick And Easy For All.* https://www.binance.com/en/blog/42149982468490 1797/Binance-Convert-Making-Crypto- Transactions-Quick-and-Easy-for-All

Printed in Great Britain
by Amazon